MY COMPANIONS ARE IN DARKNESS

DEVOTIONAL READINGS

ON PSALM 88

TYLER WATSON

My Companions are in Darkness: Devotional Readings on Psalm 88

Copyright © 2013 Tyler Watson

All Rights Reserved

Cover photograph and design by Tyler Watson.

To my Bible teachers, from Sunday school and summer camp through college, seminary, and beyond:

Thank you for introducing me to this amazing collection of books and reminding me of God's revelation contained within it.

CONTENTS

OPIUM VS. SMELLING SALTS

Karl Marx famously declared, "Religion…is the opium of the people," in which fantasies of a soothing God and a disembodied ecstasy in Heaven are given to drug people so that they might remain numb to the reality of their current suffering.[1] We can look at the history of the Christian Church, including at some contemporary sermons, worship songs, and books and see that Marx had a point—the Christian message has, at times, been watered down to a set of feel-good affirmations that deny the reality of suffering and death. Such a diluted faith can offer only the thinnest of blessings that do not address the fullness of the human experience. We face the temptation to anesthetize ourselves with beliefs that God only wants us to experience happiness or that this life doesn't ultimately matter, rather than truly wrestle with God in the midst of the confusion and pain that each of us experiences and sees in others.

Thankfully the Psalms offer no opium to our suffering. In these prayer-poems we encounter the full arc of human life—joy and sadness, victory and loss, peace and fear, confidence and doubt, health and sickness, birth and death. They don't drug our pain and turmoil with flaccid promises of escape. The writers of the Psalms display keen awareness of their distress and voice their shock, fear, and anger. As readers, we do not find opiates numbing us to troubles. The Psalms instead act like smelling salts, waking us up to the reality of life's complexity and to the God who is with us through it all.

Some psalms praise God when all is right with the world (e.g., Psalm 8). Other psalms offer thanks to God for bringing salvation and setting the world back in order when things have gone wrong (e.g., Psalm 34). We are likely most familiar and most comfortable with these first two types of psalms. But there is a third type of psalm that cries out to God when trouble arises, when enemies attack, when God seems distant, when the world is not as it should be. These lament psalms complain,

---

[1] Karl Marx, *A Contribution to the Critique of Hegel's "Philosophy of Right,"* translated by Annette Jolin and Joseph O'Malley, (New York: Cambridge University Press, 1970), 131.

protest, and wail before Yahweh, the God of Israel. We are likely not as familiar with these psalms despite the fact that there are more lament psalms than there are psalms of praise or psalms of thanksgiving. The reason for our unfamiliarity lies in the fact that the psalms of lament challenge us. They challenge our conceptions of the kinds of prayers God accepts. They challenge our images of God protecting us from every hurt and loss. They challenge our understanding of what it means to be in covenant with the God of the universe. The psalms of lament do not deny the existence of suffering—instead, they place that suffering before God's face and demand, "What are you going to do about this?"

Psalm 88 is one of the darkest and most intense prayers of lament in the whole Bible. The psalmist accurately describes suffering and the confusion it brings while teaching us a way to speak to God when we experience turmoil. This little guide will help you prayerfully read through Psalm 88 in eighteen days. The people of Israel and the Church have used the Book of Psalms as their prayer guide and hymnal throughout history. The Psalms have much to teach us about prayer if we simply slowed down and allowed their poetry to usher us into a world that deals directly with the joys and sorrows of life as well as the God who is immediately available.

As you read and pray, bring your whole life forward. If you face trouble and question where God is, let the words of Psalm 88 shape your prayers. Walter Brueggemann writes, "Psalm 88 is a defiant, buoyant prayer that relentlessly holds God accountable for experiences of trouble and at the same time holds God in hope of what God will yet do."[2] If you do not find yourself in the same place as the psalmist, remember when you were troubled and when God seemed distant and callous to your suffering, or think of those who are in turmoil and pray this psalm along with them. Come and allow Psalm 88 to act as smelling salts to wake you up to the real trouble and confusion in the world. Come pray with God's people, calling out to the God who is our only hope for salvation.

---

[2] Walter Brueggemann, "The Psalms as Prayer," in *The Psalms and the Life of Faith,* ed. Patrick D. Miller (Minneapolis: Fortress Press, 1995), 62.

THE GUIDE TO THIS GUIDE

This guide is divided into a few parts. The main section, beginning on page 21, contains questions and reflections for daily readings of Psalm 88. The Method describes the technique of meditatively reading through Psalm 88 in eighteen days.

"Faith Needs Lament" on page 9 explores the necessity of prayerful protest, how faith without lament is thin and weak, and how lament strengthens our covenant relationship with God.

"Reading Devotionally, or: Going to Half Dome, Too" on page 13 details why I think it is important to read the Bible devotionally, prayerfully, and meditatively, as well as how this method differs from other important ways of reading Scripture.

"Reading in Solitude, with the Community" on page 15 describes the temptation of reading individualistically when we read devotionally, as well as offers some suggestions on how to keep ourselves in the community of God even as we read in solitude.

For those who are like me and find the technical and historical aspects of Scripture spiritually enriching, I have also included an appendix at the end of this guide, beginning on page 45. "Textual, Historical, and Cultural Details" speaks to some of the background of Psalm 88 and how it fits into the Book of Psalms. I put this section at the end since knowledge of these matters is not necessary for the disciplines of this guide and might prove unhelpful for those who find such details distracting. I have, however, included it for those of us who love such information.

THE METHOD

This method of meditative reading will take you through Psalm 88 in eighteen days. The heading of the psalm is not included in the readings, but it is addressed in the appendix.

- **Open** the time by finding a place where you will not be distracted. Quiet yourself with some deep breaths. Pray for God—Father, Son, and Holy Spirit—to guide you through this time of reading.
- **Read** Psalm 88 in its entirety. Take your time. Do not focus on anything in particular, but let the psalm draw you into its world of turmoil and protest. Read aloud if that is helpful.
- **Meditate** on the verse of the day. Read this verse several times until you can say it from memory and then recite it a few more times. Does a phrase or word stick out to you? Pay attention to how you feel. Does this verse trouble you? Confuse you? Give you a sense of community? How do you relate to it? What longing or desire do you feel? The questions in the guide are written in the first person—ask them in first person.
- **Reflect** on the verse by using the questions in the guide if they are helpful. If God is showing you something not addressed in the questions, stay with that—do not feel like you need to follow the guide verbatim. I suggest having a journal and pen to record your insights and thoughts.
- **Respond** to God based on your reflections. Offer a prayer of lament to God for the turmoil you face. Pray for those who endure confounding pain now.
- **Read** Psalm 88 again in its entirety, this time in light of the insight you gained through focusing on that day's one verse.
- **Close** with the *Gloria Patri*, or Glory Be:
    Glory be to the Father, and to the Son, and to the Holy Spirit;
as it was in the beginning, is now, and ever shall be, world without end. Amen.

MY COMPANIONS ARE IN DARKNESS

As you read, notice repeated words, images, and themes. The psalmist describes his desperation using different evocative images. Chew on those specific words. Offer your thoughts to God.

You may find yourself memorizing Psalm 88 as you repeat these verses several times. I encourage doing this. I now find myself praying these words when God seems distant, or when I think of those I know who currently suffer.

FAITH NEEDS LAMENT

The desperation contained within Psalm 88 shocks us. Though the Psalms are the original songbook of God's people, it is doubtful that many of us have ever sung a song like Psalm 88 during a worship service or mass. The descriptions of the psalmist's turmoil are raw. Many readers will be uncomfortable with the idea of blaming and lamenting to God in the manner of the psalmist.

To our detriment, we have largely lost the discipline and tradition of lament. Without lament, we no longer act as full covenant partners with God. When two parties are in covenant with each other, if one party has not fulfilled their commitments, the other party calls them to account. When the only prayers we have at our disposal are praise and thanksgiving, we lose that ability to call Yahweh, our covenant partner, to account when we encounter suffering.[3]

While the protests and accusations in Psalm 88 may seem like the psalmist no longer trusts God, the opposite is true. Lamentation requires a robust faith. In fact, it is precisely when we think we cannot protest or complain to God that we run the risk of losing our faith. What do we do when we face terror and suffering if we cannot lament? Should we celebrate cancer? Should we praise God for hurricanes that kill people and destroy homes? If all we have to say to God in the midst of chaos are words of praise and thanksgiving, we will eventually face a choice: either delude ourselves into thinking that our turmoil does not actually exist, or walk away from this God who either does not care about our suffering or seems incapable of helping us.

The lament psalms offer us another way and show how faith can grow when all seems dark and chaotic. In protesting to God, laments affirm that Yahweh is in control while calling God to be faithful to promises previously made. Lament psalms question and complain because they believe that Yahweh is supposed to be good, loving, and faithful. Brueggemann reminds us, "the lament makes an assertion about

---

[3] Brueggemann explores the necessity of lament in a covenant relationship in his essay, "The Costly Loss of Lament," in *The Psalms and the Life of Faith*, 98-111. This essay is the finest work on lament and its implications for the faith of God's people I have ever read.

God: that this dangerous, available God matters in every dimension of life."[4] A faith without the discipline of lament is paper thin, easily destroyed by the fires and floods we will face. It is a faith that puts God in a box because it says God can only be found when we are happy. Such a faith also limits our ability to be honest with Yahweh. A faith with the discipline of lament is thick and can mature in the midst of confusion and hurt. It is a defiant faith, unwilling to let go of God, even when there is little evidence at the time confirming God's faithfulness.

Because the psalmist has cried out to Yahweh every day without any response and his unrelenting desperation ends in darkness, it would be reasonable for readers to think Psalm 88 is devoid of hope. I would argue that the psalmist still has hope, however frail it might be. The hope I see in Psalm 88 is revealed in the fact that the psalmist has not given up on crying out to God for help despite not receiving confirmation that God is even listening. The psalmist does not direct this complaint about God to another person or to "the air at random."[5] He continues to bring his complaint directly to God because he believes that God is the only hope he has for his situation to improve. If the psalmist had truly given up hope, he would have likely stopped praying his lament.

Many people have discovered that Yahweh's acceptance of lament saved their faith and offered them hope when loved ones died, when they lost jobs, when natural disasters hit, or when they suffered injustice. They did not have to just grin and bear their pain, but could cry out to God for help. In the midst of their protests, God met them again.

Readers who are not in a place of such overwhelming pain like the writer of Psalm 88 may find the psalmist's prayerful accusations of God too harsh. But those who have experienced or currently endure the kind of depression seen in this psalm may find encouragement knowing that you are not alone. Other people have been angry with God. Other people have felt abandoned by their loved ones and even by God. Suffering has a terrible capacity to make us feel distant from everyone else. Depression creates a sensation of isolation. That is certainly what we find in Psalm 88. For those who currently experience depression and loneliness, know that you have a community of fellow travelers who shared your turmoil both in the writer of Psalm 88 and in the countless people of faith who have read this psalm and discovered words prayerfully describing their pain. Know that asking Yahweh, "Why do you hide your face from me?" (Psalm 88.14b) is a perfectly valid prayer that God accepts.

---

[4] Ibid., 108. Emphasis in the original.
[5] John Calvin, *Commentary on Psalms*, Kindle Edition, location 19550.

Let us remember the social function of the Psalms as well—they intend to shape the community of God's people, not merely give us personal prayers. Just as each of us needs to relearn the discipline of voicing our laments to God when we encounter the chaos of the world, we also need to relearn the discipline of joining with others in their laments. Lamenting together, lamenting on behalf of others creates community. Praying laments with those who suffer may help ease their isolation.

Entering the dark waters of Psalm 88's laments will challenge and change us. Such is the result of wrestling with our covenant partner, Yahweh. My prayer is that through mediating on these verses we would begin to recover the accepted and required discipline of lament. As we learn to lament, may we encounter this "dangerous, available God" in new and deeper ways.

READING DEVOTIONALLY, OR: VISITING HALF DOME, TOO

For many years in the West, scholars have investigated the Bible using the tools of historical, archeological, and anthropological studies. These modern techniques have produced wonderful insights since the books of the Bible are historical documents coming to us from particular times, places, and people. To read the Bible only in that academic manner, however, misses its grandeur. To read the Bible with only one method would be like going to Yosemite Valley and staring only at El Capitan. You could awe at its mammoth granite face and it would be a fulfilling experience, but if you never walked around, or even turned to the right, you would completely miss Half Dome, Yosemite Falls, the Royal Arches, and all the other geological and biological wonders that make Yosemite Valley such a majestic place. If reading the Bible using modern critical methods is like looking at El Capitan, then employing a meditative method is like looking at Half Dome. Both methods, and others as well, are needed to appreciate any piece of Scripture's grand scope.

This guide is intended to help readers engage the Psalm 88 meditatively and devotionally.[6] To put it another way, this guide is not a Bible study. To read devotionally means using a different set of muscles. In devotional reading we do not keep Scripture at arm's length, trying to remain objective. The meditative method suggested in this guide means ruminating on Scripture, chewing on it over and over again, bringing it into our bodies so that it becomes a part of us. Reading devotionally means giving control to the Holy Spirit to guide us.

My hope is that this guide will help you encounter this amazing psalm in a manner that allows God to shape your mind and heart. When people teach others to read the Bible for personal growth, they often suggest readers ask something like,

---

[6] Some readers may wonder if the method I suggest is the practice of *lectio divina*, or divine reading. Roman Catholic and Eastern Orthodox Christians have practiced that ancient way of prayerfully reading Scripture for centuries and it has recently gained prominence among Protestant Christians, which I believe is wonderful. Anyone familiar with that practice will know I am clearly indebted to it, but I would hesitate to call my suggested method *lectio divina* in any proper sense.

13

MY COMPANIONS ARE IN DARKNESS

"How do I apply this passage to my life?" I appreciate the value behind this question, namely that the message of Scripture is alive and has much to say about how we live today. I fear, however, this is the wrong question because it seems like we are trying to take the message of the Bible and conform it to our situations.

I believe we need a different posture toward biblical texts. Rather than going to the Bible for a helpful message we can fit into our lives, we should turn to the Bible expecting to encounter God's revelation, which calls us to change how we live with God and with our neighbors. Let us receive Scripture's invitation to transform our thoughts and choices in order to align our lives with the biblical stories of creation, redemption, and new creation. Therefore our guiding question will not be, "How can I apply this psalm to my life?" but, "How does my life fit into the story of this psalm?"

Let us remember, however, that no one way of reading can fully comprehend the Bible's breadth and depth. Thus devotional reading is not without its shortcomings. For example, as we focus on only one verse each day, we may feel tempted to take that verse out of context. That is why each day we will read all of Psalm 88 twice—once at the beginning and once at the end.

READING IN SOLITUDE, WITH THE COMMUNITY

This method of devotional reading demands solitude, which may unintentionally encourage us to read Psalm 88 individualistically, as if it only affects me and my life. It is true, we read devotionally because we believe God is speaking to us personally, in our unique situations. We believe Jesus wants to shape each of us to be more like him. I encourage us to find ourselves in Psalm 88. When the verses say, "I," really think of this as your testimony. Always remember, however, that the Bible's books, including the Psalms, were written to shape the community of God's people. There may be no one around us as we read, or we may not speak with anyone during each day's devotions, but we are always with the people of God throughout history and around the world whenever we open Scripture and let the word of Yahweh form us.

When I was a student in seminary, our preaching professors taught us to ask ourselves an important question during sermon preparation. In the midst of biblical exegesis, writing, and rehearsing, we were to ask who else did we need to be in the room with us? Our instructors meant we ought to be aware of the issues and experiences shaping the lives of the people to whom we preached the Bible as well as how those Scriptures spoke to them. As devotional readers, we should ask a similar question. Not only do we ask, "God, what are you saying to me through this passage?" We also ask, "Who else needs to hear this passage?" Bring to mind others who endure turmoil and depression. Allow these verses to shape not only your prayers to God, but also your actions in the world. Bring your whole self to Psalm 88—your thoughts, emotions, desires, fears, as well as your relationships, family, communities, vocation, neighborhood, and ecosystem.

PSALM 88

A Song. A Psalm of the Korahites. To the leader: according to Mahalath Leannoth. A Maskil of Heman the Ezrahite.

1   O LORD, God of my salvation,

      when, at night, I cry out in your presence,

2   let my prayer come before you;

      incline your ear to my cry.

3   For my soul is full of troubles,

      and my life draws near to Sheol.

4   I am counted among those who go down to the Pit;

      I am like those who have no help,

5   like those forsaken among the dead,

      like the slain that lie in the grave,

like those whom you remember no more,

      for they are cut off from your hand.

6   You have put me in the depths of the Pit,

      in the regions dark and deep.

7   Your wrath lies heavy upon me,

      and you overwhelm me with all your waves.   *Selah*

8 You have caused my companions to shun me;

      you have made me a thing of horror to them.

   I am shut in so that I cannot escape;

9   my eye grows dim through sorrow.

   Every day I call on you, O LORD;

      I spread out my hands to you.

10 Do you work wonders for the dead?

      Do the shades rise up to praise you?   *Selah*

11 Is your steadfast love declared in the grave,

      or your faithfulness in Abaddon?

12 Are your wonders known in the darkness,

      or your saving help in the land of forgetfulness?

13 But I, O LORD, cry out to you;

      in the morning my prayer comes before you.

14 O LORD, why do you cast me off?

      Why do you hide your face from me?

15 Wretched and close to death from my youth up,

      I suffer your terrors; I am desperate.

16 Your wrath has swept over me;

      your dread assaults destroy me.

17 They surround me like a flood all day long;

      from all sides they close in on me.

18 You have caused friend and neighbor to shun me;

my companions are in darkness.

DAILY DEVOTIONAL READINGS ON PSALM 88

DAY & VERSE 1

Open. I quiet myself and pray for God—Father, Son, and Holy Spirit—to guide me through this time of reading.

Read. I read all of Psalm 88.

Meditate. I read the selection of the day several times, slowly.

> *O LORD, God of my salvation,*
>
> > *when, at night, I cry out in your presence*

Reflect.

"Salvation" can carry several meanings—welfare, deliverance from harm, protection from physical, social, or spiritual oppression.

> *Which definition of "salvation" most resonates with me today? What salvation might I need today? Who do I know that is suffering that might need salvation? Why does the psalmist begin by declaring Yahweh is the "God of my salvation"? When I am troubled, in my seasons of sadness and confusion, where do I go seeking salvation?*

I imagine the psalmist awake at night crying out to Yahweh.

> *Is the psalmist awake because his pain and worry prevent him from sleeping? Is the psalmist awake because he will not sleep until he receives an answer from Yahweh? When have I had sleepless nights and what kept me awake? What were my middle-of-the-night prayers?*

Respond. I offer a prayer to God for myself and for others informed by my reflections.

Read. I read all of Psalm 88 again.

Close. I end this devotional by praying the Glory Be:

> Glory be to the Father, and to the Son, and to the Holy Spirit;

as it was in the beginning, is now, and ever shall be, world without end. Amen.

DAY & VERSE 2

Open. I quiet myself and pray for God—Father, Son, and Holy Spirit—to guide me through this time of reading.

Read. I read all of Psalm 88.

Meditate. I read the verse of the day several times, slowly.

> *let my prayer come before you;*
>
> > *incline your ear to my cry.*

Reflect.

> *Why would the psalmist ask for his prayer to reach Yahweh? Can I remember a time when God did not seem to listen to my prayers? In retrospect, how did that experience feel? Do I think that Yahweh has heard my prayers lately? What prayers have I offered recently that seem to have gone unheard?*

Respond. I offer a prayer to God for myself and for others informed by my reflections.

Read. I read all of Psalm 88 again.

Close. I end this devotional by praying the Glory Be:

> Glory be to the Father, and to the Son, and to the Holy Spirit;

as it was in the beginning, is now, and ever shall be, world without end. Amen.

DAY & VERSE 3

Open. I quiet myself and pray for God—Father, Son, and Holy Spirit—to guide me through this time of reading.

Read. I read all of Psalm 88.

Meditate. I read the verse of the day several times, slowly.

> *For my soul is full of troubles,*
>
> > *and my life draws near to Sheol.*

Reflect.

> *How am I doing emotionally, mentally, spiritually, and physically? Do I feel full of troubles to my core, like the psalmist? If not, can I remember a time when I did feel full of troubles? As I think of these troubles, what do I want to say to God?*

Sheol is understood to be a nonphysical place where the dead go and where God does not intervene.[7]

> *Have I ever thought that God was not at work in my life? What did I think and feel when I did not see Yahweh acting as I hoped? Where do I long to see God's intervention in the world, in the lives of my friends and family, in my life?*

Respond. I offer a prayer to God for myself and for others informed by my reflections.

Read. I read all of Psalm 88 again.

Close. I end this devotional by praying the Glory Be:

> Glory be to the Father, and to the Son, and to the Holy Spirit;
>
> as it was in the beginning, is now, and ever shall be, world without end. Amen.

---

[7] John Goldingay, *Psalms Vol 2: Psalms 42-89*, Baker Commentary on the Old Testament Wisdom and Psalms (Grand Rapids: Baker Academic, 2007), 705.

DAY & VERSE 4

Open. I quiet myself and pray for God—Father, Son, and Holy Spirit—to guide me through this time of reading.

Read. I read all of Psalm 88.

Meditate. I read the verse of the day several times, slowly.

> *I am counted among those who go down to the Pit;*
>
> *I am like those who have no help,*

Reflect.

> *What might the psalmist be experiencing that he would say he is considered like the dead who have no help from anyone—not from friends, not from family, not from God. Do I feel similarly helpless today, or have I ever confronted such helplessness? How might I use the psalmist's prayers when I encounter suffering? How might I pray for and help others who are in distress?*

Respond. I offer a prayer to God for myself and for others informed by my reflections.

Read. I read all of Psalm 88 again.

Close. I end this devotional by praying the Glory Be:

> Glory be to the Father, and to the Son, and to the Holy Spirit;

as it was in the beginning, is now, and ever shall be, world without end. Amen.

DAY & VERSE 5

Open. I quiet myself and pray for God—Father, Son, and Holy Spirit—to guide me through this time of reading.

Read. I read all of Psalm 88.

Meditate. I read the verse of the day several times, slowly.

> *[I am] like those forsaken among the dead,*
>
> > *like the slain that lie in the grave,*
>
> *like those whom you remember no more,*
>
> > *for they are cut off from your hand.*

Reflect.

> *How well do I relate to the psalmist's description of being forsaken, forgotten, and cut off? Can I remember an experience of being forgotten by someone I loved, whether a friend or family member? Can I stay in that memory for a moment, no matter how painful it might be? How would I describe that experience? What would it be like for God to no longer remember me, to cut me off from Yahweh's hand, that is, to cut me off from Yahweh's power and protection?*

Respond. I offer a prayer to God for myself and for others informed by my reflections.

Read. I read all of Psalm 88 again.

Close. I end this devotional by praying the Glory Be:

> Glory be to the Father, and to the Son, and to the Holy Spirit;

as it was in the beginning, is now, and ever shall be, world without end. Amen.

DAY & VERSE 6

Open. I quiet myself and pray for God—Father, Son, and Holy Spirit—to guide me through this time of reading.

Read. I read all of Psalm 88.

Meditate. I read the verse of the day several times, slowly.

> *You have put me in the depths of the Pit,*
>
> *in the regions dark and deep.*

Reflect.

The psalmist shifts from describing his turmoil to now accusing Yahweh for bringing on his troubles.

> *How does this verse challenge or conform to my understanding of God? What do I think about the psalmist's accusation that God is the cause of his loneliness and lifelessness? How comfortable am I with charging God with bringing on some of the troubles in my life? What does the psalmist's accusing Yahweh say about his faith in God?*

Respond. I offer a prayer to God for myself and for others informed by my reflections.

Read. I read all of Psalm 88 again.

Close. I end this devotional by praying the Glory Be:

> Glory be to the Father, and to the Son, and to the Holy Spirit;

as it was in the beginning, is now, and ever shall be, world without end. Amen.

DAY & VERSE 7

Open. I quiet myself and pray for God—Father, Son, and Holy Spirit—to guide me through this time of reading.

Read. I read all of Psalm 88.

Meditate. I read the verse of the day several times, slowly.

> *Your wrath lies heavy upon me,*
>
> > *and you overwhelm me with all your waves.*   Selah[8]

Reflect.

I imagine Yahweh's wrath lying heavy upon me. I imagine the sensation of God's anger overwhelming me like waves in the ocean.

> *What does Yahweh's heavy wrath feel like? How do I respond to being overwhelmed by God? Do I think God is angry with me today? How does this verse challenge my understanding of a patient and loving God? Is it possible for me to find comfort in this verse—and in this psalm as a whole— knowing that someone else has felt rejected by God? Is there someone I know who might feel like God is overwhelming them with wrath? What do I want to say to God?*

Respond. I offer a prayer to God for myself and for others informed by my reflections.

Read. I read all of Psalm 88 again.

Close. I end this devotional by praying the Glory Be:

> Glory be to the Father, and to the Son, and to the Holy Spirit;

as it was in the beginning, is now, and ever shall be, world without end. Amen.

---

[8] The Hebrew word *selah* appears in many psalms, but its meaning and function have been largely lost to us. It shows up at the end of lines on occasion with no discernible pattern. It may have had a liturgical or musical purpose, but we cannot be sure. The NRSV chooses, therefore, simply to transliterate the word rather than translate it. See: Goldingay, *Psalms Vol 2: Psalms 42-89,* 704.

DAY & VERSE 8

Open. I quiet myself and pray for God—Father, Son, and Holy Spirit—to guide me through this time of reading.

Read. I read all of Psalm 88.

Meditate. I read the verse of the day several times, slowly.

> *You have caused my companions to shun me;*
>
> > *you have made me a thing of horror to them.*
>
> *I am shut in so that I cannot escape;*

Reflect.

The psalmist's loneliness grows more complete as he not only suffers distance from God, but also abandonment from loved ones.

> *Have I ever been shunned by my loved ones, the people who are supposed to be near me when I hurt? Have I ever experienced loneliness so intense and complete that it feels like being imprisoned? Do I feel that way now or can I bring those memories and emotions to mind as if I am experiencing them today? Can I speak to God as the psalmist does? Do I know someone suffering this kind of loneliness today and how may I reach out to them?*

Respond. I offer a prayer to God for myself and for others informed by my reflections.

Read. I read all of Psalm 88 again.

Close. I end this devotional by praying the Glory Be:

> Glory be to the Father, and to the Son, and to the Holy Spirit;

as it was in the beginning, is now, and ever shall be, world without end. Amen.

DAY & VERSE 9

Open. I quiet myself and pray for God—Father, Son, and Holy Spirit—to guide me through this time of reading.

Read. I read all of Psalm 88.

Meditate. I read the verse of the day several times, slowly.

> *My eye grows dim through sorrow.*
>
> *Every day I call on you, O Lord;*
>
> *I spread out my hands to you.*

Reflect.

> *Can I relate to the psalmist's exhaustion from his sorrow? After all the intense accusations against God, why does the psalmist still call on Yahweh? Are the psalmist's hands spread out in a request for help, or in exasperation, or both? What do the psalmist's actions say to me when I am exhausted from distress? How can I pray for others who have been calling out and reaching out to Yahweh for a long time without an answer?*

Respond. I offer a prayer to God for myself and for others informed by my reflections.

Read. I read all of Psalm 88 again.

Close. I end this devotional by praying the Glory Be:

> Glory be to the Father, and to the Son, and to the Holy Spirit;

as it was in the beginning, is now, and ever shall be, world without end. Amen.

MY COMPANIONS ARE IN DARKNESS

DAY & VERSE 10

Open. I quiet myself and pray for God—Father, Son, and Holy Spirit—to guide me through this time of reading.

Read. I read all of Psalm 88.

Meditate. I read the verse of the day several times, slowly.

> *Do you work wonders for the dead?*

> *Do the shades rise up to praise you?* Selah

Reflect.

"The shades" refers to the powerless, ghostlike inhabitants of Sheol.

The psalmist continues to accuse Yahweh now using a series of rhetorical questions.

> *What tone do I read in the psalmist's questions? What emotions do I imagine him feeling as he makes these inquiries of God?*

The psalmist seems to say that his suffering to the point of death would be worthless, even for Yahweh, since if he were dead, the psalmist would be unable to be in relationship with God—receiving and witnessing God's wonders and returning thanks for Yahweh's intervention.

> *What experience do I have with suffering—suffering either I endure or witnessed in others—that seems pointless and worthless? What questions do I want to ask of God about this suffering?*

Respond. I offer a prayer to God for myself and for others informed by my reflections.

Read. I read all of Psalm 88 again.

Close. I end this devotional by praying the Glory Be:

> Glory be to the Father, and to the Son, and to the Holy Spirit;

as it was in the beginning, is now, and ever shall be, world without end. Amen.

DAY & VERSE 11

Open. I quiet myself and pray for God—Father, Son, and Holy Spirit—to guide me through this time of reading.

Read. I read all of Psalm 88.

Meditate. I read the verse of the day several times, slowly.

> *Is your steadfast love declared in the grave,*
>
> > *or your faithfulness in Abaddon?*

Reflect.

Abaddon, like Sheol mentioned in verse 3, is a netherworld related to the grave, where the dead go and where God is not active.[9]

> *What tone do I read in the psalmist's questions? What emotions do I imagine him feeling as he makes these inquiries of God? Does the psalmist see any purpose to his turmoil? What do I think of the psalmist's accusation that God causes his suffering?*

The psalmist longs to experience Yahweh's steadfast love and faithfulness.

> *Can I imagine God's deep, committed love and faithfulness absent from my life? What would my life look like without them? In what areas of my life or in the world do I long to see God's steadfast love manifested? Is it an ongoing physical ailment? An addiction or sin that lingers in my life? Injustice? A broken relationship? The ongoing oppression of people on the margins by the powerful?*

Respond. I offer a prayer to God for myself and for others informed by my reflections.

Read. I read all of Psalm 88 again.

Close. I end this devotional by praying the Glory Be:

---

[9] Marvin E. Tate, *Vol. 20: Psalms 51–100*, Word Biblical Commentary (Dallas: Word, Incorporated, 1998), electronic ed.

MY COMPANIONS ARE IN DARKNESS

Glory be to the Father, and to the Son, and to the Holy Spirit;

as it was in the beginning, is now, and ever shall be, world without end. Amen.

DAY & VERSE 12

Open. I quiet myself and pray for God—Father, Son, and Holy Spirit—to guide me through this time of reading.

Read. I read all of Psalm 88.

Meditate. I read the verse of the day several times, slowly.

Are your wonders known in the darkness,

or your saving help in the land of forgetfulness?

Reflect.

What tone do I read in the psalmist's questions? What emotions do I imagine him feeling as he makes these inquiries of God?

I remember a time when I saw or experienced God's wonders.

Can I now imagine what life would be like to be cut off from those wonders?

I remember a time when I received saving help from God.

Can I now imagine what life would be like without that salvation?

Respond. I offer a prayer to God for myself and for others informed by my reflections.

Read. I read all of Psalm 88 again.

Close. I end this devotional by praying the Glory Be:

Glory be to the Father, and to the Son, and to the Holy Spirit;

as it was in the beginning, is now, and ever shall be, world without end. Amen.

DAY & VERSE 13

Open. I quiet myself and pray for God—Father, Son, and Holy Spirit—to guide me through this time of reading.

Read. I read all of Psalm 88.

Meditate. I read the verse of the day several times, slowly.

> But I, O LORD, cry out to you;
>
> > in the morning my prayer comes before you.

Reflect.

The psalmist returns to his protest.

> *What prayers for help and salvation have I offered to Yahweh that have gone unanswered? What do I do when I see no response to my prayers? Do I give up praying? Do I look to someone or something else for help? Do I continue bringing my requests and protests to Yahweh? After enduring such painful silence, why does the psalmist keep going to Yahweh? What does the psalmist's persistence reveal about his faith?*

Respond. I offer a prayer to God for myself and for others informed by my reflections.

Read. I read all of Psalm 88 again.

Close. I end this devotional by praying the Glory Be:

> Glory be to the Father, and to the Son, and to the Holy Spirit;

as it was in the beginning, is now, and ever shall be, world without end. Amen.

DAY & VERSE 14

Open. I quiet myself and pray for God—Father, Son, and Holy Spirit—to guide me through this time of reading.

Read. I read all of Psalm 88.

Meditate. I read the verse of the day several times, slowly.

> *O LORD, why do you cast me off?*
>
> > *Why do you hide your face from me?*

Reflect.

> *Do I think God has cast me off? Do I believe that God should cast me off? What would I say to God if I could be in God's presence?*

I recall an experience of being rejected and the feelings that came with it.

> *Now can I imagine Yahweh rejecting me? What would that loneliness feel like? How much more intense would the loneliness and rejection feel if God also hid from me so that I could not find Yahweh? Who might believe that Yahweh has cast them off and how may I pray for them today?*

Respond. I offer a prayer to God for myself and for others informed by my reflections.

Read. I read all of Psalm 88 again.

Close. I end this devotional by praying the Glory Be:

> Glory be to the Father, and to the Son, and to the Holy Spirit;

as it was in the beginning, is now, and ever shall be, world without end. Amen.

MY COMPANIONS ARE IN DARKNESS

DAY & VERSE 15

Open. I quiet myself and pray for God—Father, Son, and Holy Spirit—to guide me through this time of reading.

Read. I read all of Psalm 88.

Meditate. I read the verse of the day several times, slowly.

> Wretched and close to death from my youth up,
>
> I suffer your terrors; I am desperate.

Reflect.

> What is it like to see death around every corner? Can I relate to these statements from the psalmist? What in my life helps me or prevents me intimately understanding this verse? If the psalmist has been close to death since his youth, why would he call Yahweh the God of his salvation in verse 1?

I think of those who have been close to death their whole lives such as those living in slums and war zones, or those born with chronic illnesses, or those enduring ongoing oppression, or those who do not have regular access to life's basic necessities.

> How might people living in those circumstances pray to God? Can I join them in their prayers?

Respond. I offer a prayer to God for myself and for others informed by my reflections.

Read. I read all of Psalm 88 again.

Close. I end this devotional by praying the Glory Be:

> Glory be to the Father, and to the Son, and to the Holy Spirit;

as it was in the beginning, is now, and ever shall be, world without end. Amen.

DAY & VERSE 16

Open. I quiet myself and pray for God—Father, Son, and Holy Spirit—to guide me through this time of reading.

Read. I read all of Psalm 88.

Meditate. I read the verse of the day several times, slowly.

> *Your wrath has swept over me;*
>
> > *your dread assaults destroy me.*

Reflect.

> *What memories and emotions come to mind when I read this verse? What questions does it raise in me? What do I think angers God? Do these accusations ring true with my experience of Yahweh? Does this verse comfort me, knowing that someone else has endured a season of feeling rejected by God?*

Respond. I offer a prayer to God for myself and for others informed by my reflections.

Read. I read all of Psalm 88 again.

Close. I end this devotional by praying the Glory Be:

> Glory be to the Father, and to the Son, and to the Holy Spirit;

as it was in the beginning, is now, and ever shall be, world without end. Amen.

DAY & VERSE 17

Open. I quiet myself and pray for God—Father, Son, and Holy Spirit—to guide me through this time of reading.

Read. I read all of Psalm 88.

Meditate. I read the verse of the day several times, slowly.

> They surround me like a flood all day long;
>
> from all sides they close in on me.

Reflect.

The psalmist refers to Yahweh's "dread assaults" from verse 16. I imagine for a moment God's wrath surrounding me like a flood that does not diminish.

> What does it feel like to be this troubled? What would my day consist of if I experienced God's assaults drowning me, surrounding me all day long? How can someone continue to exist in the midst of such pain and agony? What could possibly bring the psalmist some relief? What would a lifeline be for him?

Respond. I offer a prayer to God for myself and for others informed by my reflections.

Read. I read all of Psalm 88 again.

Close. I end this devotional by praying the Glory Be:

> Glory be to the Father, and to the Son, and to the Holy Spirit;

as it was in the beginning, is now, and ever shall be, world without end. Amen.

DAY & VERSE 18

Open. I quiet myself and pray for God—Father, Son, and Holy Spirit—to guide me through this time of reading.

Read. I read all of Psalm 88.

Meditate. I read the verse of the day several times, slowly.

> *You have caused friend and neighbor to shun me;*
>
> *my companions are in darkness.*

Reflect.

The psalm ends in darkness with the psalmist reiterating his utter loneliness.

> *What experience do I have with feeling rejected and utterly alone? What brings me comfort when I am in that loneliness? Do I feel close and connected to loved ones today? What do I think of the psalmist saying God is causing his friends to shun him? Where is consolation in these seasons of terror? Where is hope? Where is God?*

Respond. I offer a prayer to God for myself and for others informed by my reflections.

Read. I read all of Psalm 88 again.

Close. I end this devotional by praying the Glory Be:

> Glory be to the Father, and to the Son, and to the Holy Spirit;

as it was in the beginning, is now, and ever shall be, world without end. Amen.

FINAL REFLECTIONS

You have now spent eighteen days swimming in the dark waters of Psalm 88. This psalm challenges our understanding of God's goodness. Because Yahweh accepts these laments, the psalm also makes new types of prayer available to us. Take some time to look back on your experience with this psalm. Consider the following questions. You might answer one or two that stick out to you, or simply let them be a springboard to start your own reflections. You might even write your own psalm of lament.

- Consider the experience of reading a piece of Scripture slowly and repetitively. What insights did you gain through spending so much time with Psalm 88 that you may have missed had you read it more quickly? What was most helpful about this method? What was the least helpful?

- In what ways did you find yourself relating to this psalm? In what ways did you find it difficult to relate to it?

- Before walking through this psalm, what did you think about offering laments to God? Were you comfortable with protesting to God when you faced suffering, depression, loneliness, or confusion?

- After engaging Psalm 88 in this manner, what do you think about lamenting to God?

- What unjust circumstances in your life or in the lives of people you love do you want to protest? What laments do you want to offer God?

- Going forward, how do you want to incorporate lament more into your prayer life? How do you want to incorporate lament more into the life of your faith community?

- In what ways can this psalm open your eyes to the suffering of others and how can you pray laments on their behalf? How might you reach out to those enduring helplessness and depression?

MY COMPANIONS ARE IN DARKNESS

Please receive this final blessing:

Remember that Yahweh, the God of our salvation is available to you.

Lift up your protests, raise your shouts, ask your questions.

May Yahweh answer you and save you,

And may you keep protesting until Yahweh does answer.

Amen.

APPENDIX

TEXTUAL, HISTORICAL, AND CULTURAL DETAILS

The Book of Psalms has long been the prayer book and hymnal of the people of Israel and the Christian Church. Any student of the Psalms must keep this religious function in mind as they perform their analysis. Biblical studies in recent centuries have sought to explore Scripture with the tools of historical and scientific inquiry and these endeavors have, to a large extent, enriched our understanding of the Bible—its language and the cultures from where it emerged. This small guide is devotional in nature and therefore my hope is that the even the analytical discussion of Psalm 88 would be faithful to this psalm's intention, namely, that through its words we would find our voice and have an honest experience of prayer.

CLASSIFICATION

Biblical scholars have spent much energy classifying the 150 psalms and agree on three large categories: praise, lament, and thanksgiving.[10] Psalm 88 clearly falls into the category of lament. Further, this psalm fits into the subgenre of a lament for an individual as opposed to a lament for a (national) leader or a lament for the congregation.[11]

---

[10] Judaism, Roman Catholicism, and Protestantism all include 150 psalms. Eastern Orthodox traditions accept 151 psalms. Though there is general consensus on the three large categories of psalms, scholars differ widely in classifying the number of sub-categories.

[11] Psalms lamenting for an individual include: Psalms 6, 10, 22, 26, 31, 38-40, 42-43, 54-59, 64, 70-71, 86, 88, 109, 120, 141-142. Psalms lamenting for a leader include: Psalms 3, 5, 7, 13, 17, 25, 28, 35, 61, 63, 69, 102, 140, 143. Psalms lamenting for the congregation include: 12, 44, 60, 74, 79, 80, 83, 85, 89-90, 94, 106, 123, 126, 137, 144. I have borrowed both Goldingay's threefold categories and catalogue of lament psalms as found in "OT500: The Writings as Introduction to the Old Testament, Syllabus and Course Notes," Pasadena: Fuller Theological Seminary, 2010.

Laments for an individual generally contain certain elements, giving us a pattern for our prayers when we suffer. (1) The psalm opens with an address or invocation to God, reminding us that this is a prayer directed to God in pursuit of a change in the situation, not the psalmist merely blowing off steam. (2) The psalmist then offers a lament about or directed toward three subjects: the speaker who offers protests about his situation; God, who is accused of either ignoring the psalmist or bringing about the psalmist's suffering; the enemies inflicting pain on the speaker. (3) Then the psalmist affirms his trust in Yahweh. (4) The psalmist offers his request for attention and deliverance. (5) The psalmist then makes a significant turn and offers a vow to praise God—usually in public—once the deliverance is complete. (6) Finally, the psalmist thanks God in advance for the salvation that is sure to come.[12] We should note that not every lament for an individual will contain each of these elements, just that they are indicative of the subgenre as a whole.

While Psalm 88 fits squarely with other psalms of lament as it cries out to God for salvation, it also holds a unique place in the Bible for what it is missing. Let us contrast Psalm 88 to Psalm 71, another psalm of individual lament. The writer of Psalm 71 spends a good amount of time complaining to God, but then offers the typical vow of praise and thanksgiving: "My lips will shout for joy when I sing praises to you; my soul also, which you have rescued" (71.23). Though the writer of Psalm 71 is currently in turmoil, he praises God and offers thanksgiving as if Yahweh has already rescued him. We find no turn to praise and no thanksgiving in Psalm 88. This lack of characteristic praise makes Psalm 88 challenging. More than any other piece of Scripture—aside from perhaps some proclamations of Job or Jesus' cries of agony on the cross—the speaker comes close to utter despair. The psalmist cries out to Yahweh for rescue, but as readers we get the sense it is a cry of desperation, of being completely at the end of one's rope. What little hope we find contained within is faint.

STRUCTURE

Psalm 88 may be broken into three sections, corresponding with the three times the psalmist invokes Yahweh's name in verses 1-2, 9b, and 13-14. The content of these three sections are not radically distinct from each other, but each plays a variation on the psalm's desperate theme. In the first section (v.1-9a), the psalmist begins by

---

[12] Craig C. Broyles, "Lament, Psalms of," in *Dictionary of the Old Testament: Wisdom, Poetry, and Writings*, eds. Tremper Longman III and Peter Enns (Downers Grove, IL: IVP Academic, 2008), 387-388.

invoking Yahweh and begs for his prayer to reach God's ears. Coupled with the later complaints of crying out for long periods, we get the sense that the psalmist wonders if God is even paying attention. Then the psalmist lays out the lament. Through evocative imagery of the Pit, Sheol, and the grave, he communicates he is suffering to the point of death. What is more, the psalmist blames God for his pain. In the second section (v.9b-12) the protest takes the form of a series of rhetorical questions whose assumed answers are all, no. The psalmist's demise due to his afflictions would not be good for him, for Yahweh, or for the community. The psalmist continues to use bleak imagery to convey that he is agonizing to the point of death. In the final section (v.13-18), the psalmist again levies his protest much like in the first section—he is near death, God laid these afflictions on him, God is nowhere to be found, and the psalmist is utterly lonely. Because Psalm 88 never makes a turn to praise God as do other lament psalms, the prayer only grows more desperate to the point that it ends in darkness.[13]

The psalmist articulates the experience of suffering in frightening terms, giving us a window into his psychological and spiritual distress. If we were to try to reconstruct the psalmist's story, however, we would quickly realize that he intentionally does not supply us with important information. "Notice that even though there is great detail, one cannot determine from the Psalm what the actual problem is—whether sickness, abandonment, guilt, imprisonment. The poet has an amazing capacity to say much and yet leave everything open. Thus the Psalm provides a marvelous receptacle which we are free to fill with our particular experience."[14] Once again we see Psalm 88's religious function in that it teaches us how to pray. If we knew that the psalmist suffered from a terminal illness, we might think we could never pray these words unless we also had a terminal illness. But because Psalm 88 is not specific at this one point, we can fit our lives into the story this psalm no matter what type of suffering we experience.

PSALM 88'S HEADING: AUTHORSHIP AND CULTURAL CONTEXT

"A Song. A Psalm of the Korahites. To the leader: according to Mahalath Leannoth. A Maskil of Heman the Ezrahite."

---

[13] In fact, in the Masoretic Text, upon which all modern English translations are based, the Hebrew of verse 18 simply reads, "My companions…darkness." Goldingay, *Psalms Vol 2: Psalms 42-89*, 643 n.7 and Tate, *Vol. 20: Psalms 51–100*, electronic edition.

[14] Brueggemann, *Praying the Psalms*, 33.

I did not include this heading of the psalm in the daily readings though it is the first verse in Hebrew manuscripts as well as in current Jewish Publication Society verse numbering. The headings found in many of the psalms contain information that often confuses readers, including scholars who spend much time studying these texts. Still, the headings help us devotionally because they remind us of the earthy and human character of Scripture. The books of the Bible are deeply cultural products, though not merely cultural products. They emerge from specific and real people in specific and real places as they lived with God. The psalms' headings show that people and communities wrote, edited, collected, and handed down these prayer-poems.

Psalm 88 has one of the longest headings in the Book of Psalms.[15] Despite its length and detail, the heading's terms are not immediately clear. Devotional readers should not get stuck trying to decipher the exact meaning of the heading. I will not discuss the heading thoroughly, but if readers would like to know more, the commentaries listed in the bibliography will supply them with helpful information. I will highlight a few points.

The heading tells us that this is a song to be sung, though as I said in "Faith Needs Lament," I doubt many of us have ever sung a song like this in a modern worship service. The songs of contemporary North American churches consist mostly of praise and thanksgiving. We would do well to recapture the discipline of lament in our music. Coming together to sing African-American Spirituals, many of which contain the wrestling with God we find in psalms of lament, would be a great place to start. Arranging the lament psalms to music for congregational singing would also help. Singing protests to God does not put barriers between us and Yahweh. Instead, as we sing laments, we stand with the generations of God's people in relationship with Yahweh.

Exodus 6.21-24 says the Korahites were descendants of Levi through Kohath and Izhar. As a family they had a role in leading the Hebrew people in religious observance. According to 2 Chronicles 20.19, the Korahites were a company of singers at the Temple.[16] Many readers will assume that Heman the Ezrahite is the author of this final version of Psalm 88, but this may not necessarily be the case. 1 Kings 4.31 mentions Ethan the Ezrahite and Heman as famous wise men who served during Solomon's reign in the tenth century BC. 1 Chronicles 25.5-6 describes Heman as involved in leading musical worship. It seems possible that if Heman and the Korahites were involved in leading worship at the Temple, they could have had a hand in creating this psalm, though further shaping by later editors is highly

---

[15] Goldingay, *Psalms Vol 2: Psalms 42-89*, 645.
[16] Tate, *Vol. 20: Psalms 51–100*, electronic edition.

probable.[17] Psalm 88 gives us no real clues as to when it was written as the headings of psalms could have been added later during periods of redaction or even as the collection of the Book of Psalms was being finalized, somewhere around the fourth century BC.[18] Broyles shows us the value of the long process that shaped individual psalms and the Book of Psalms as a whole:

> The psalms were hammered out over generations of living with God. We moderns should not impose upon them our assumptions that individual, private experience is to be valued more highly than the experience of God reflected in a corporate identity. In fact, they are what generations of the believing community have found to be appropriate and effective ways of speaking to God. The worshiper who recites a psalm speaks not with a singular voice but rather with the voice of generations of God's people. This should give greater confidence when speaking to God. In addition, we are invited to read our own personal experience against the wider experience of the community and so see that our experiences are shared by others.[19]

Let us not bog ourselves down in questions about authorship and dating. Because so much of this historical data has been lost to us, questions around these matters may distract readers more than they illuminate the text. We may find ourselves stuck as we try to decipher who wrote what. Worse, we might forget to read the passage, missing what God wants to say to us. A psalm's power does not depend on who wrote it, but on the truth of what it says about life with God.

HOLDING TOGETHER THE PSYCHOLOGICAL AND RELIGIOUS, THE PERSONAL AND COMMUNAL

In one of the earliest Christian studies on the Psalms, the Early Church Father, Athanasius of Alexandria, writing in the fourth century, offers a key insight:

> Among all the books, the Psalter has certainly a very special grace, a choiceness of quality well worthy to be pondered.... It is like a picture, in

---

[17] Goldingay, *Psalms Vol 2: Psalms 42-89*, 645.

[18] For the date of the Book of Psalms, see: Peter C. Craigie with Marvin E. Tate, *Vol. 19: Psalms 1-50* (2nd ed.), Word Biblical Commentary (Nashville, TN: Nelson Reference & Electronic, 2004), electronic ed.

[19] Broyles, "Lament, Psalms of," 385-386.

which you see yourself portrayed, and seeing, may understand and consequently form yourself upon the pattern given.... You find depicted in it all the movements of your soul, all its changes, its ups and downs, its failures and recoveries.[20]

In the majority of Scripture, God speaks to us. In the Psalms, we speak to God. Because of their personal nature as prayer-poems, the psalms—and the lament psalms in particular—invite psychological readings. Through them we gain deep insight into the organic relationship between Yahweh and people. Within their verses we find responses to the whole of human experience.

The lament of Psalm 88 is individual as opposed to corporate, further inviting psychological interpretations.[21] The psalm also serves a religious function and we must hold this together with its psychological aspects. John Calvin captures the psychological and liturgical purposes of Psalm 88 when he says the psalmist, "recites the agony which he suffered from the greatness of his sorrows, yet his purpose was at the same time to supply the afflicted with a form of prayer."[22] The psalm is not merely an account of personal distress, but also a prayer given to members of the community when they suffer. Psalm 88 gives us words to say to God when we are so afflicted that we cannot muster prayers on our own.

The psalms of lament, even those lamenting for an individual, are not to be prayed only in solitude. They have a communal function as well. Scholars note that most of the psalms of lament would not likely be used by the people of ancient Israel during regular liturgies—either at the set daily prayers or the congregational litanies during specific seasons and festivals such as Passover. These psalms would more likely be prayed when specific needs arose.[23] Though the use of the lament psalms was more situational, they were still used in corporate worship, when the community gathered together to sing, pray, and listen to Scripture.

The psalms of lament may be prayed by individuals in distress or by communities in need. They may also be prayed by a community standing in solidarity with a fellow member experiencing turmoil. Psalm 88 gives us words to say to God on behalf of

---

[20] Athanasius of Alexandria, "A Letter of Athanasius, Our Holy Father, Archbishop of Alexandria to Marcellinus on the Interpretation of the Psalms." *Athanasius: The Life of Antony and the Letter to Marcellinus*, translated by Robert C. Gregg (New York: Paulist Press, 1980), 101-129. Retrieved from: www.athanasius.com/psalms/aletterm.htm

[21] Brueggemann says Psalm 88 can be seen as an account of, "severe depression." *Praying the Psalms: Engaging Scripture and the Life of the Spirit*, 2nd ed. (Eugene, OR: Cascade Books, 2007), 33.

[22] Calvin, *Commentary on Psalms*, Kindle Edition, location 19540.

[23] Broyles, "Lament, Psalms of," 385.

others who are so afflicted that they can barely pray for themselves. How would our congregations need to change in order to recapture the practice of lament when we gather to worship? What shape would our witness to the world take as we stand with those suffering injustice and protest to God together?

BIBLIOGRAPHY

Athanasius of Alexandria. "A Letter of Athanasius, Our Holy Father, Archbishop of Alexandria to Marcellinus on the Interpretation of the Psalms." In *Athanasius: The Life of Antony and the Letter to Marcellinus*. Translated by Robert C. Gregg, 101-129. New York: Paulist Press, 1980. Retrieved from: www.athanasius.com/psalms/aletterm.htm

Broyles, Craig C. "Lament, Psalms of." In *Dictionary of the Old Testament: Wisdom, Poetry, and Writings*. Edited by Tremper Longman III and Peter Enns, 384-399. Downers Grove, IL: IVP Academic, 2008.

Brueggemann, Walter. "The Costly Loss of Lament." In *The Psalms and the Life of Faith*. Ed. Patrick D. Miller, 98-111. Minneapolis: Fortress Press, 1995.

————. *Praying the Psalms: Engaging Scripture and the Life of the Spirit*, 2nd ed. Eugene, OR: Cascade Books, 2007.

————. "The Psalms as Prayer." In *The Psalms and the Life of Faith*. 33-66.

Calvin, John. *Commentary on Psalms*. Kindle Edition.

Craigie, Peter C. with Marvin E. Tate. *Vol. 19: Psalms 1-50* (2nd ed.). Word Biblical Commentary. Nashville, TN: Nelson Reference & Electronic, 2004. Electronic Edition.

Goldingay, John. "OT500: The Writings as Introduction to the Old Testament, Syllabus and Course Notes." Pasadena: Fuller Theological Seminary, 2010.

————. *Psalms Vol 2: Psalms 42-89*, Baker Commentary on the Old Testament Wisdom and Psalms. Grand Rapids: Baker Academic, 2007.

Marx, Karl. *A Contribution to the Critique of Hegel's "Philosophy of Right."* Translated by Annette Jolin and Joseph O'Malley. New York: Cambridge University Press, 1970.

Tate, Marvin E. *Vol. 20: Psalms 51–100*. Word Biblical Commentary. Dallas: Word, Incorporated, 1998. Electronic Edition.

ACKNOWLEDGEMENTS

Brian Eyer, Sherry Walling, Carey Watson, and Brian Wright looked at a draft of this devotional. I would like to thank them all for their encouragement, suggestions on content, and help in editing this guide.

ABOUT THE AUTHOR

Tyler Watson is a stay-at-home dad living in the Bay Area of northern California with his wife and son. Prior to his current vocation he served as a pastor in congregations of the Evangelical Covenant Church. He received his Master of Divinity from Fuller Theological Seminary.

He is also the author of the devotional, *Delivered from All My Fears: Devotional Readings on Psalm 34.* He blogs at The Space Between My Ears (spacebetweenmyears.com).

Made in the USA
Middletown, DE
10 January 2023

21812132R00035